MAKE ROOM FOR THE MIRACLE

By Russ Cherry

Never! Ever! Give Up!

Russ Cherry

ISBN 10: 0692502343
ISBN 13: 9780692502341

Mom and Dad—without your faith,
there would be no miracle.

Colleen, you <u>are</u> my miracle.

Josh and Emily, always remember to look for miracles.

--R.C.

CHAPTER ONE

I was going to fly jets.

Not just any jets, but the fastest jets the world had ever seen.

It wasn't a dream or a goal. It was my plan.

It was a plan that began when I was 11 and we went to the Air & Space Museum. I was instantly fascinated and from that moment knew that I'd someday be strapped in a cockpit, flying Mach 5 and soaring through the clouds like a man on fire.

My grandparents bought me the commander book for the space shuttle, which came complete with the launch sequence. I was in heaven, and I had it memorized within days. Suddenly it wasn't just jets I'd fly. I'd fly in space.

In my teens I began taking lessons at Walker Air Force Base, which had been the largest base of the Strategic Air Command during the Cold War. There was no feeling like it; it was where I was meant to be.

I had perfect eyesight. I was the right height. I was strong. I had the grades. I was going to the Air Force Academy, and no one would ever tell me otherwise.

But first, I had to finish high school.

And before then, I had to get to football practice.

THE POWER OF A DREAM.

Most kids have dreams of one kind or another. Maybe, like me, it was to be a pilot and an astronaut. For others, it could be a fireman or professional basketball player or a dancer on Broadway or a racecar driver or a teacher. Dreams captivate, inspire and often motivate—even when those dreams change.

I believe dreams are incredibly powerful because in them lies hope. Hope for what we can be, what we can do, what we can achieve. Although dreams may change— and they often do—their power remains consistent.

Without dreams, the world's greatest businesses would never have been built. Inventions would never have been created. People would never learn or try to be anything different than what they have always been. We'd probably still be living in caves somewhere, wondering when something to eat would wander our way instead of coming up with a way to go out and get it for ourselves.

While that may seem far-fetched, I want you to think about those areas of the world—perhaps even of the country or city in which you now live—in which poverty is most evident. In these communities, dreams and hope are pretty hard to find. Most teens aren't wondering what college they should go to; they are just focused on getting a job that pays the bills. Graduation rates are low and crime rates are high. Dreams, and options, seem few and far between.

That's why I tell people not to just dream—but to dream big. Really big. Whether you're a child, an adolescent or an adult, think about something bigger than the right now. Consider what could be, and let yourself run wild when it comes to following your dream.

In my own life, living without a dream would have just been existing. I would never have gotten up the courage to ask my wife Colleen on a date, much less ask her to marry me. I also would never have written this book, because I would probably be slaving away in a cubicle somewhere, despising what I was doing but feeling like there was no other choice. I would never have gone into business for myself or started sharing my story or discovering how people and organizations can think and communicate and function better.

One caveat: achieving your dream takes more than just thinking about it. You have to take action, and you have to prepare for the reality that when you're making your dreams happen obstacles will always get in your way. Just remember: it's part of the process. Don't let those tough moments stop you from doing something truly amazing.

CHAPTER TWO

Taking a hit is part of the game. But some hits are harder than others.

Practice that day was grueling. The heat of August, the sweat dripping off our faces. Roswell, New Mexico in the summer is not a forgiving place, especially when you're running drills twice a day to get ready for the first game of the season.

One drill. Another.

One hit. Another. And another.

I didn't avoid it. I dug in. I wasn't going to be defeated. Not in practice. Not ever. This was my year. My season.

Then I noticed this bump on my neck. It was swelling— and it kept swelling. It wasn't super painful, but it grew bigger with every minute that passed.

As I dragged myself home, I realized what had happened. I'd fractured my collarbone. Frustrated, I wondered why it happened now. Why so close to our season opener?

I showed my parents who called our family doctor. As we sat in his office, he leaned in to examine the spot. He didn't say anything at first. When he did, I wished he hadn't.

"It's Hodgkins," he said. "You have cancer."

That day was the last time I put on my football pads. The season was over.

It was the hardest hit I'd ever taken.

LEANING IN.

My junior year of high school was something I had really looked forward to. My brother Jon had been a great athlete, and it's always hard to live in your brother's shadow. Now that he was heading to college, it was finally my turn to show what I could do. I had trained hard, I was strong and I was excited.

I also truly loved the game of football. I loved the feel of the grass. I loved the sound of pads hitting. I loved how the crowd sounded, and certainly didn't mind looking at the cheerleaders (hey—I was a teenage boy!) I loved to tackle people. I even didn't mind getting tackled as long as I'd run the play the way I was supposed to.

That isn't to say that football was easy. I'd played the game for years, and I knew the downsides. You learn early on there only gets to be one winner, and I didn't like not winning. I didn't like the pulled muscles or the bruises or the jammed fingers.

My high school football coach was a great guy— someone I had a lot of respect for. He could walk into a locker room and take boys getting rousted by the opposing team and make them into giants by the time they retook the field.

One of his favorite mantras was "Tough times don't last, but tough people do." Of course, now I know that's from a book published in the mid-80's by Robert Schuller, but I didn't at the time. All I knew was that if our coach told us we could get through something, we could. We could play in the heat, we could play in the mud, we could play through the pain, we could do whatever we needed to because he believed we were that strong. And eventually we believed it too.

My coach also taught me something important about football, and that's how to take a hit. People who haven't played football often don't understand how any player can pop back up off the field after getting brought down hard. There's actually a science to it.

It begins with good conditioning, building strength to allow you to withstand what comes at you. It's also often better to lean into a hit, absorbing it rather than trying to tighten up or brace against it. Most importantly, after you take the hit, you get up, shake yourself off and you get back in the game.

I didn't expect to get cancer before I had my first girlfriend. I didn't expect to get cancer at all. But if there's one thing that football taught me, it's that I could take a hit. It was a part of the game. You've undoubtedly recognized that I made it through. And part of the reason, as you'll learn as you continue to read this book, is that I learned how to lean in to the hits that came my way.

Things are going to happen in your life. It's a part of the game, the plan—whatever you want to call it. Sometimes you'll get hit by little things that will annoy you. Other times, you'll get knocked around by something that will take the wind right out of you and you'll have to lay there for awhile, trying to catch your breath. You may see it coming or it could take you by surprise.

Whatever that hit is that you take, recognize you're stronger than it will ever be. Know you have more power than it does. Then shake yourself off and get back in the game.

CHAPTER THREE

"This will hurt."

I'd always been an active kid, and I'd had my share of falls, scrapes and fix ups. I was an athlete; pain was an expected part of the game. I'd been hurt before. This couldn't be that different.

And I was tough. How bad could it be?

The doctor explained that a biopsy was needed to see whether my cancer had spread. I would lie on the gurney and he would use lidocaine to numb the skin. He'd make a small incision, place the needle into my hip and extract the marrow. It would be quick, but uncomfortable.

I removed my shirt and pants, laid on the gurney and looked over at my dad, who was standing next to me. I felt the sting of the lidocaine, the doctor told me he was making the incision.

I was ready.

And then I wasn't.

The pain shot through my body as needle met bone. As the doctor pressed harder, the pain intensified accordingly. My hands gripped the cold metal of the gurney, and it began to bend and lift under the pressure. I looked at my dad again; he looked nauseated and he began to sway as the color drained from his face.

The pressure increased as the needle was shoved so hard it passed through the back of the bone. The doctor pulled it back, and as he began to suck the marrow into the tube, I began to hyperventilate. Suddenly it felt as if electricity was coursing through my nerves, and I stared at my fingers, believing they would literally blow off at any minute.

The doctor withdrew the needle. I lay shaking on the table, tears falling from my eyes.

He waited a moment as my shaking subsided, and allowed me to regain my breath. I began to sit up, but he placed his hand on my clammy skin.

"Now," he said, "it's time to do the other side."

EVERYONE HAS A NEEDLE.

I like to think that somewhere in the world there is someone who has lived without worries or cares, without pain, without those moments that bring them to their knees, but the fact is, I know better. Everyone, no matter how good they may be at hiding it, has to face a needle. They will experience physical or (perhaps more likely) emotional pain. The kind of pain that they once never knew existed.

It could be the loss of a job. The breakup of a marriage. Finding out a spouse has been unfaithful. The death of a loved one. Losing a child. Learning they have cancer.

To this day, people ask me which was worse: facing that needle the first time, when I didn't know what to expect, or facing it when I knew what was to come. There are many who reason that when you know what to expect, you can better prepare for it.

While I advocate there are steps you can take to mitigate difficulties in life, I truly don't believe that people should spend their lives focused on preparing for bad things to happen. Of course it's a good idea to save money so that you have reserves to support you if you lose a job. Getting a good education or learning a trade is a must in my book—you need to be able to support yourself. I have a life insurance policy (yes, they gave me one) because I want my wife and children taken care of when I can no longer be there for them.

But no one should live his or her life waiting, preparing for and focused on the worst that could occur. Because when you do, you lose the many opportunities that can come from facing your needle.

Had I possessed an inkling of what was to come before I climbed in the car that day to drive to Albuquerque, I wouldn't have gone. I would have said no. I would have run from it, as far as I could run. I would have told them I didn't care if the cancer had spread.

Instead I found myself lying on that now-twisted table, my body vibrating with fear, now knowing what was to come. I tensed every muscle. The needle had an even more difficult task as the doctor tried to drive it into my back. The pain was, if possible, more intense as, once again, the electrical currents flew through my nerves and my fingers began to burn. Later, as my father drove us the three hours back from Albuquerque to Roswell I lay in the backseat sobbing, my face turned into the upholstery. I was bruised and broken and feeling utterly devastated.

But I also learned, in that moment, that I had reservoirs of strength I never before knew I possessed. I knew that if I could get through that experience, I could get through anything.

And I believe you can too.

In that moment when you are feeling as though you cannot survive one more moment of the pain you are experiencing, know you can get through it. When your heart and body are aching, you can and will stand again. It's okay to feel sad, to mourn, to allow yourself to experience the physical or emotional pain you're feeling. The process is an incredibly human experience, one that refines us.

You, too, have strength within you that right now you may not realize you have. Strength that will get you through your own experience and through any others that may come.

CHAPTER FOUR

"My life is over."

It was all I could think about as I stared blankly at the television screen. As I would lie on my bed. As I wandered down the halls of our house. There was nothing left for me. Everything I'd ever dreamed of was gone.

Kids my age don't get cancer. Nobody I knew had cancer. Just me. I was alone, and I was hopeless.

The house was quiet, and I was glad. I was miserable, and I wanted everything and everyone to feel the same way.

My dad came home and walked into the family room, my own personal cave of despair. He stood in the doorway, watching me. I slowly looked up at him and saw the wealth of emotions that crossed his face.

Then I watched as the man—my rock, my hero—took in a deep breath. His shoulders seemed to slump and his head dropped.

"No Dad," I silently pleaded. "Don't give up on me too. If you give up then I really will know it's over."

Then in that moment his head raised and I saw a flash of something I'd never seen before in his eyes. I braced myself, but what followed was not what I could ever have expected.

His voice was powerful, and it came from somewhere deep within his soul. Two words. Just two words. But they were two words that changed my life.

"Do something!" he bellowed. Then he turned around and left the room.

DOING SOMETHING.

My dad is a great man. The older I get, the more I recognize it, especially now that I am a father myself.

He could have stood in that doorway and cried right along with me. He could have joined in my pity party. He could let me know that wallowing in my sadness was exactly what needed to happen.

Instead, he looked at his son, lying on a couch. A son who was strong and muscular, who had the ability to fight cancer. He knew, by that time, that if you were going to get a cancer diagnosis, the one to get was Hodgkins. The survival rate is astronomical compared to other types of cancer. This is a disease you can win against with proper care and treatment.

Was he worried? Of course he was. Did he wonder about his son's future? Every parent does, whether their child has cancer or not. But he was more worried about having me lie there, having me give up, than he was worried about the cancer cells that were doing their darndest to ruin my day.

Now you might think that it would have been better for him to walk over, put his hand on my shoulder and gently say "Russ, I believe that you'll make it through this. Your mom and I will be there every step of the way. I want to encourage you to live your life to the fullest in every way."

But my father knew me. He knew the swirling dervish of a teenage mind. He knew that he had to walk into my pity party, take down the balloons and toss the refreshments out the window. He needed me to take action.

So he told me to do something. And I listened.

I admit that as he left the room I had no idea of what exactly I was supposed to do. But somewhere within me there was this little spark that made me want to find out. It took me some thinking (again—teenage boy here) to recognize I didn't have to let cancer ruin every aspect of my life. And the aspect I decided was most important in that moment was pizza.

So I called my buddy and we talked about pizza. By the end of our conversation, he'd convinced me that I shouldn't just order a pizza (my favorite food in all the world) but that I should start delivering it. He said he made decent money doing it and got free food on top of it. It seemed like the ideal situation (have I pointed out the teenage mind yet?)

Keep in mind that when you have cancer there are usually treatments involved that tend to affect, in one aspect or another, your outward appearance. My parents knew this and, as a pre-emptive strike against hair loss caused by the radiation that was ultimately prescribed to treat the disease, had me take my senior pictures just as my junior year was underway. The front of my hair was pretty much unaffected. The sides and back, however, took on a distinctive look of their own. I also dropped a little weight, which made my clothes hang on me.

I'm pretty sure that the people who opened their door—especially considering we lived in the UFO capital of the planet Earth—thought that some form of alien had landed on their steps. Sometimes I got really good tips, although I still wonder if they felt sorry for me or just didn't have small enough bills on them to tip less and wanted me to get off their front step before the neighbors saw me instead of waiting for me to make change.

I didn't really care, because I was doing something. I was living my life—for as long a life as I had left.

So my question to you is this: are you doing something? If not, I can ask my dad to come for a visit.

CHAPTER FIVE

Our old blue Skylark piled on the miles.

It was just over 400 miles round trip between Roswell and Albuquerque. We'd travel almost three-and-a-half hours each way for a 30-second dose of radiation. I came to know every inch of it as my parents—usually my mom—drove me back and forth to my treatments for the next five months.

On the way there, I looked out the front window. Sometimes, I was strong enough to drive. On the way back, there were times I dangled out the passenger window, vomiting as we went.

When I was feeling okay, I'd deliver pizzas at night, people looking strangely at the kid the weird haircut. I was still strong, I was still standing. I was doing something. The miles kept piling up.

In December, we arrived at the oncology center to meet with the doctors. A quick examination, a review of my last images, and I was officially declared cancer free.

As we headed home in the Skylark, I knew I should feel relieved. The doctors said I was cured. It was time to start living my life again as a "normal" kid.

But deep inside, I knew something wasn't right.

And that's when the real journey began.

LISTENING.

When I was a kid, my mother would always remind me that before crossing the road I needed to stop, look and listen. I'm guessing it's not exactly exclusive to my mother, but it's something that always stuck out in my mind. Why? You see, the stopping I totally understood after about the age of 3—running out into traffic was not a good idea. "Look" was also something I comprehended as well. See what's coming down the road, see what dangers exist close to you. But the "listen" part escaped me.

What was I supposed to listen for? Birds? Dogs? My friends who lived down the street from our home? Then my mom explained that you can sometimes hear a vehicle coming long before you see it. Listening was part of keeping me safe.

As my treatments came to an end and the doctors told me to head back to my normal teenage life, everything looked okay. They didn't see anything out of the ordinary at that point, and to tell you the truth, neither did I, with the exception of my radiation-produced hairstyle. But even though I looked okay on the outside—and on the inside, according to my doctors—I almost felt a sense of dread.

At first I thought it was a fear that the cancer would return. I'd heard of people who got into car accidents and even years later would feel anxious whenever they saw another vehicle approach an intersection. I knew, however, that Hodgkins was a one-and-done kind of cancer; my doctors assured me I could never get it a second time.

So I tried to get back to being a teenage kid. I started back in school, worked delivering pizzas at night and tried to do anything but listen to that voice inside me that kept trying to warn me that something wasn't okay, no matter what the doctors said.

As you will soon learn, I needed to listen better. I needed to listen to that voice that was telling me there was something wrong with my health—just like I needed to listen to my dad when he told me to do something. I'm not sure if it would have made a difference in terms of what was going to happen, but it could have made what I would face easier.

People describe that "voice" in a lot of different ways, often based on personal beliefs. They may refer to it as a feeling, a prompting, a still small voice, a sense or an inspiration.

No matter what you may personally call it, if you're feeling something's a little "off" in your life, I strongly encourage you to take the time to listen, as listening may guide you to take a certain course of action. You may be inspired to get into—or out of—a situation. You may recognize that you need to start looking for a new job, or be prompted to stay where you are right now.

Listening can change your life. It might even save it.

Are you listening?

CHAPTER SIX

I had a lot of questions.

I was at the top of a ski hill, looking out at the valley beneath me. We'd traveled to Utah—then billed as having "the greatest snow on earth" and it had delivered on the promise. But despite my love of skiing, I was exhausted. I couldn't help but wonder—yet again—what was wrong with me.

It was March of 1988, the end of ski season and three months since I'd been told I was cancer-free. I wanted to get one more run in. It was a beautiful day, but something felt wrong. I'd been losing weight, no matter how much I ate. I'd been lifting in the gym for months, but I couldn't build any muscle. The fatigue was grueling.

What was happening?

I just wanted to get in one last run.

Could I make it down?

By the time I made it to the bottom of the slope, every breath was in agony. My lungs ached, and I was shaking. I kept trying to shake it off, but nothing was helping.

How long is this going to last?

I climbed into the car with my family, and my cousins suggested we go get pizza. When we arrived at the restaurant, I shocked everyone when I said I wanted to stay in the car. I curled up in the back seat, covered with any coats or blankets I could get my hands on. The spring sun streamed in through the windows.

Why couldn't I get warm?

My parents decided we needed to cut our trip short. Before we left they called our physician, and we drove the 17 hours back to Roswell as quickly as possible. My temperature soared and my body shook. I could see the concern on my parents' faces.

Did they know something I didn't?

One test. Then another.

The doctor came into the room and sat down across from me. He looked me in the eye.

"You have pneumonia," he said. "You also have Stage 4D lung cancer."

One diagnosis. Three thoughts:

1. Did the people around me know I loved them?
2. Had I made a difference?
3. I didn't want to die.

WHAT REALLY MATTERS.

When I learned about my second diagnosis, everything went white. Not in a heavenly, ethereal sort of way, but in the sense of everything simply disappearing. I didn't see anything. I didn't hear anything. Everything was just gone.

Except those three thoughts.

In those 16 years that had been my life, had I shown the people I cared about how much I loved them? Did they know how I felt about them, how much I appreciated them? Had I told them what they meant to me? If time stopped now, would they question it?

I also wondered whether my life had mattered. It wasn't about ego—that "are people going to cry when I'm gone" sort of thing. It was mattering in the truest sense of the word. Had I done enough good? Had I built other people up, been kind to the kids I went to school with, gone out of my way to be a good person? Had I made a difference?

Then there was the "d" word: dying.

I wasn't afraid of death because I've always believed it's just a natural part of life. But I didn't want to die. I knew that I wouldn't live my dream of going to the Academy or becoming an astronaut at this point. I had too many health issues. But I wanted to go to college. I wanted to see the world. I wanted to get married, to be a dad. I wanted to see what life held. I wanted to beat this even though at the moment I could barely breathe.

Too often I think we get caught up in all the other stuff. We have to live in the right house in the right neighborhood and park just the right car in our driveway. We need to make enough money at the right kind of job and keep up—or surpass—our friends and family and colleagues in terms of what we have or what we earn or the accomplishments we achieve. We put our kids in every activity under the sun, then run from one place to another without really spending time together. It's about our image more than who we truly are.

When those "big" moments happen in life, you start to see what really matters. I've heard stories of people who have lost their home due to a fire, flood or natural disaster. Their first concern is whether or not their family is okay. Then it's their pets. But then what they're most concerned about are things like photographs and home movies—things with little or no monetary value. Why? Because those are the things that tell their stories, proved they lived, captured their best memories.

You may have had an experience that underscored what was truly important in your life. If not, I'd challenge you to consider precisely what would matter most to you if you were sitting in a room and had a doctor deliver what is realistically a terminal diagnosis.

Would you think about the house you live in or would you think about the people who live there with you?

Would you want to drive right back to your job or would you want to find your best friend and talk for hours about what he or she means to you?

If everything you thought was important were gone tomorrow, what would really matter?

CHAPTER SEVEN

"Take him home. Make him comfortable. Prepare to say goodbye."

The room was white and cold and silent. He tried to be gentle as he told my parents to prepare for my death. But it didn't feel that way. Nothing could make it feel different than what it was. I was going to die. Plan the funeral. Say your farewells. That's all that's left.

But then I heard my father's voice.

"What are our options?"

Options? The doctor explained there weren't options. I weighed 93 pounds. I was weak. I had double pneumonia, with both lungs full of fluid. I couldn't breathe. My right lung was full of cancer. If they'd caught it earlier, maybe they could have done something. But there wasn't really anything that they could do at this point.

Again came my father's voice, this time even stronger.

"We need options. Give us an option."

In lung cancer cases they recommend chemotherapy. But I was at Stage 4D. It doesn't get worse than that. The recovery rate was almost non-existent, and the outcome with or without treatment would likely to be the same.

"So there's something we can do. There is an option."

I looked at my father. He wasn't saying I wasn't going to die. He just wasn't going to accept that I would die without a fight.

Shaking his head, the doctor relented. Surgery would be required to complete a biopsy and determine the course of treatment needed. They would have to open my chest, crack open my ribs. My lung would likely have to be removed. If I came off the table—and that was a big if—then chemotherapy would follow. Chemotherapy I wasn't likely to survive.

"We'll take him home. When is the surgery?"

THE ADVOCATE.

Until I was 16-and-a-half I never knew what an advocate was. Even then I didn't have a word to explain what my father had just done. How he had stepped in between me and my doctor and negotiated for my life.

My friends who are attorneys and those who work in the legal system understand the concept of advocacy. In a court of law, there are always two sides of an issue whether it's a civil one or a criminal one. Each side is represented by an advocate—someone who speaks on their behalf. Just like my father did for me in that examination room.

You see, I was just a kid. I couldn't prescribe a course of treatment for my cancer. I couldn't order surgery to be done. I didn't have the slightest clue what needed to happen. Neither, in fact, did my father. But he wasn't willing to give up—just like he hadn't been willing to let me give up those many months before.

Keep in mind that the doctor wasn't trying to be unkind. He was doing his very best to break bad news. He didn't want to see me or my parents suffer needlessly by putting me through a surgery he was sure I could never survive. He looked at the boy sitting on the table in front of him, weighing less than a hundred pounds, with a disease that people far healthier than I was die from.

He believed what he was suggesting was the kindest thing that could possibly be done and ultimately the easiest on me and for my family.

He was probably right. But kindness—and easiness—wouldn't give me a shot at life.

As a parent now of two amazing children, I am humbled by what my parents did for me that day. Their hearts, I have little doubt, were breaking. They had no desire to see me suffer. They'd watched me beat cancer before, then watched again as their "healthy" boy had deteriorated for no apparent reason. They knew I could barely breathe at this point, that my pulse was weak, that things were bleak.

But they weren't ready to give in, and they weren't about to let me give in either.

I wish everyone had someone in his or her corner, willing to negotiate on their behalf. That every man, woman and child who is facing difficulty could have someone fighting for them. That victims could be protected, the weak defended, the sick cared for.

I've also learned since that day in the examination room that sometimes you also have to advocate for yourself.

As of this writing, I've had 27 more years of life throwing a lot of curve balls my way in terms of my health, my professional life and my personal life. My parents set an amazing example for me, and I've learned that sometimes I have to stand up for myself.

Sometimes I have also had the responsibility—and the privilege—of advocating for someone else.

You may be at a point in your life where you can look back and recognize the people who have advocated for you at various times, in various places. I hope so. I hope you've had that kind of support. If not, try to remember that most people—not all, but most—do the best they can with what they have, just like the doctors who told me I was cancer-free at first.

Perhaps you're facing something extraordinarily difficult right now and recognize the need to advocate for yourself. You may even be in a position where you know you need to advocate for another person.

It may feel burdensome, and you may be afraid, but I encourage you not to be. I encourage you to stand strong, like my father, even if your heart is breaking. Don't just ask for answers—ask for options, even if it means asking time and time again.

And whatever you do, don't mistake the kind thing or the easiest thing for the right thing.

CHAPTER EIGHT

Some things in life can't be explained.

We returned home from the doctor's office that night, exhausted and unsure of what was to come. To my doctor's credit, he kept his word and set up the surgery for the next day.

I was back on the couch, this time because I couldn't sit up. The pneumonia was running its course, but somehow knowing that my lung was full of cancer made breathing even more labored. I knew I just had to make it to the next day.

Breathe in, breathe out.

I heard a knock at the door, but thought it was probably someone from our church stopping by to give support. At this point, I didn't much care who came by. I had one job.

Breathe in, breathe out.

My surgeon, Dr. Nyack, walked into the room. I wasn't sure why he was there, and from the look on my parents' faces, neither did they.

He explained that he felt compelled to come to our home that night to examine me pre-surgery. Coming to a patient's home wasn't something he usually did. From the way he said it, I got the impression he'd never done it, in fact.

Breathe in, breathe out.

He began his examination, focusing on my neck. I wasn't sure what he was doing—the cancer was in my left lung. I didn't have anything in my neck.

At least, I hadn't that morning when I had gone to the doctor.

But there they were. Visible tumors just above my left collarbone. There was a look of excitement on Dr. Nyack's face.

Breathe in, breathe out.

He knew what I didn't. He knew I could now have a local biopsy on those tumors without having to undergo life-threatening surgery to open up my chest.

It was cancer. But in this case, more cancer was exactly what was needed. Cancer was a blessing. If I could survive the night, treatment could begin within 24 hours.

There is no other way to say it. It was a miracle.

MAKE ROOM FOR THE MIRACLE.

People give up too soon.

Not every person, mind you, but far too many of them. When a challenge comes, their first instinct is to throw up their hands and say they're done.

Kids quit a sport they love because they don't get to play the position they want or get as much game time as they'd like.

Students drop out of college when course work gets more demanding.

Couples hit a rough patch in their marriage (by the way, every relationship does) and the first thing they do is head to a lawyer's office.

Entrepreneurs throw in the towel after a few months when things don't go exactly as planned, despite having dreamed of starting their own business for years.

Managers fire employees who could be amazing because of a mistake, a disagreement or a misunderstanding.

Patients get a cancer diagnosis and decide they're going to die.

There are few things that frustrate me more than when I hear about—or see—people give up too soon. It's not that I don't understand discouragement or sadness; in fact, I think I understand it better than most. I know what it means to feel despair and loss and hurt, to cry until I had no more tears to shed. To watch some of my dreams come to an end.

I will also say that in some cases, putting an end to something is not only okay, it's necessary. For instance, dysfunctional or dangerous relationships need to end quickly and safely. Employees who are disruptive to the flow of business or who jeopardize the wellbeing of colleagues need to be let go. And yes, for some patients diagnosed with a terminal disease, who have pursued every reasonable course of action, opting not to undergo further treatments may be the right choice for them.

But few people are actually in those situations. In most cases, the things they are experiencing are temporary at best, and giving up instead of holding on is a mistake.

Instead, they—you—need to make room for the miracle.

If my parents hadn't asked, time and time again, for options—if they had given up—no appointment for surgery would ever have been made. Dr. Nyack would never have come to our home. The new tumors in my neck would never have been found. Treatment would never have begun. The miracle that is my life would never have happened.

I learned another valuable lesson that night: hope matters.

I wasn't supposed to live through the night, and I'm sure that those hours were some of the longest my parents had ever endured. But we now had hope, we had options and those two things together got us through the night and through what would later come.

I will also tell you that was the just first of many miracles in my life. At this point, over two decades later, I could not possibly count the amazing things that have happened simply because I refused to give up that day or in the days, weeks and months that followed.

There will be some (there always are) who say what happened wasn't a miracle. That the tumors in my neck were there all along or that my cancer wasn't as advanced as the doctors said. Or they'll suggest that the real miracle would have been if the diagnosis was wrong or if the cancer suddenly disappeared.

I know better.

Miracles, you see, come in a lot of different shapes and sizes. And they come for a lot of different reasons. You may not always get the miracle you want, but when it happens, you'll get the one you need most.

But if you give up, it will never come.

You have to hang on, even when it's hard. You have to have hope to get through those difficult times.

You have to make room for the miracle.

CHAPTER NINE

My diagnosis was still a terminal one.

Although there was a sense of relief that came with the results of the biopsy and knowing I would begin treatment, the fact remained that I was still, for all intents and purposes, dying.

What I was about to go through next wasn't, at least at first, going to help change that.

Chemotherapy, you see, is designed to kill cells, and it does an exceptional job. Unfortunately, it takes out healthy cells right along with the cancerous ones. At less than 100 pounds, there was a very distinct reality there wasn't enough of the "healthy" me to survive the treatment.

Chemotherapy began with an IV, but I'd had plenty of those. Then came a massive dose of Decadron—the same steroid used to dope racehorses. Without it, they told me, there would be little hope I'd survive the brutal effects of the chemotherapy itself. My heart sped up wildly, and in that moment I felt I could do anything. Chemotherapy—and cancer—had no chance against me.

Then the infusion therapist walked in. He was covered from head to toe; a surgical gown, thick leather apron, face shield and thick rubber gloves. Even his shoes were completely covered. He ripped open the bright yellow bag emblazoned with a very evident "poison" mark, he pulled out the solution, hung it next to the saline, and connected the two.

I watched as it began to drip. One, then two, then three. For the first few minutes I felt fine. That came quickly to an end.

The violence of the nausea shocked me. Every muscle in my body was clenched, my stomach churning. I threw up once, then twice. Then I couldn't stop. My insides were twisting, and I was wrenching in pain. It didn't stop. Every drip of the drug seemed to signal another round. I was dripping with sweat and shaking. There was nothing left in my stomach, but it continued, waves of nausea sweeping over me, followed by dry heaves.

When the infusion was complete, the side effects weren't. For nearly 5 hours I continued to vomit every 2 to 3 minutes. Then it was every 10 to 15 minutes. By the time the 24-hour mark had hit, it was once an hour.

Two weeks later, we returned to the clinic for another round. I thought it would be easier. I was wrong. But I sat in the chair and held out my arm anyway.

Maybe I was going to die. But I was going to die trying.

MAINTAINING FOCUS.

I would love to say that after my first or second or third chemotherapy treatment I was feeling like my old self again. That just wasn't the case.

At times too weak and emaciated to walk by myself down the hallway, I would sit in the chair as greater levels of chemotherapy drugs were administered. The medical team was aggressively fighting this disease, and it felt as though they were throwing everything but the kitchen sink into my veins.

Some days I was so sick, so emaciated, that I bordered on even being conscious. I was hospitalized more than once, and there were days my illness seemed almost unconquerable. The doctor kept warning us that my prognosis was still bleak.

But I had made a decision. I was going to die trying. When I had the strength—and sometimes when I didn't—I was going to fight.

You might feel overwhelmed because of health difficulties or because of the work that's piling up on your desk or because you've just experienced a life change. You may be feeling that what you're facing is the opposite of terminal; in other words, that there's never going to be an end to what you're facing. Don't give up. You've got to keep fighting.

But how did I fight when I was so sick? I learned I had to focus on today.

I couldn't think about tomorrow or next week or next month. All I had was today, so how was I going to fight for the next 24 hours? What could I do to show my family I loved them right now? How could I make a difference today?

I also had to forget about what I couldn't do and focus on what I could.

What could a skinny sick kid practically glowing from the chemo coursing through his body do? Sometimes it was sitting up in bed. Occasionally it was finding a way to make my mom smile (I once threw up chicken noodle soup so hard I ended up with noodles hanging out of my nose, making both of us laugh until our stomachs hurt.) Other times I could actually go out and deliver pizzas with my friends or go help on a service project at my church.

But doing what you can do today isn't just a principle that applies when it comes to getting through illness. It applies to any challenge or life change like death, divorce, job changes, fractured friendships or financial loss. It also applies to those struggling with depression, addiction or other issues. Focus on today. Get through today. Do what you can and don't worry about what you can't.

Keep in mind that this idea also isn't just about getting through something. It also applies to building something. As entrepreneurs learn early, there are only so many hours in a day and your body can only go for so long without needing sleep. It's important to have a strategic plan for your business that sets milestones and allows you to look down the road a bit. But the greatest accomplishments and the most significant source of growth will come in maintaining focus on today, and doing everything you can with the time you have right now.

CHAPTER TEN

What you think about matters.

Cancer taught me many lessons, some more pleasing than others. One of them was that thoughts are things. The things you put in your mind have an impact on what you can—or can't—do.

The team at the oncology center introduced me to meditation. When I'd come in for a session, they'd play a meditation video for me in an effort to help me relax before and after my infusion.

I learned to breathe deeply, to relax my muscles, to clear my mind. But the moment I'd hear the rustling of the chemo bag, I'd be reaching for the nearest garbage can.

One day, however, I decided reaching for the garbage can at the sound of a plastic bag wasn't going to happen. And I challenged myself in the biggest, baddest way I could: by eating what I thought would be the world's worst thing to throw up.

By then I was stronger—strong enough to drive myself to my chemo treatment. On the way, I decided to stop in at Taco Bell and get one of my all-time favorite meals: Enchiritos (burritos swimming in red sauce) and a huge Mountain Dew, the largest one they had. But in my mind, it wasn't going to be a problem. I had chosen my course, and I was committed.

As I drove, I downed it all. My stomach full, I strode into the oncology center.

I sat in the chair. I began to meditate, relaxing from the top of my head to my toes. I heard the bag rustle, then rip open. I felt them connect the medicine to the port in my chest. I knew the chemo was heading into my blood stream. I consciously thought about NOT throwing up, NOT giving in to the drugs.

Nothing happened. The nausea came, but I didn't vomit.

For five minutes.

Then I reached for the garbage can and my stomach let loose. But when I came up, I was grinning.

I'd lasted five minutes longer than I ever had before. In my mind, I'd won.

THINK AND WIN.

You've probably heard about the power of positive thinking hundreds—if not thousands of times. The idea that if you think happy thoughts you will, in fact be happy. I don't know if I necessarily believe that. I mean, you can try to think happy thoughts all you want, but if your hair is on fire, you lose your job, your dog bites you and your girlfriend breaks up with you, you're not going to have a big grin all over your face.

I do, however, agree that what you think and how you think affect what happens to you in one way or another. Some people will use phrases like "self-fulfilling prophecy" or "self-efficacy." I prefer to say that thoughts are things.

If you think that you're going to fail in business, you will. If you think that you'll never overcome a challenge in your marriage, you won't. Most things in life work that way. Most times—not every time—they pretty much end up working out the way you think they will.

What do you think about yourself? What do you think about your personal situation? When you go to work are you excited and think about all of the things you can accomplish in the day ahead or do you dread it and think it will be the longest day of your career? Do you look at your spouse or significant other and think of all the great characteristics they have or do you think about all of their shortcomings? Do you think you can lose weight or start your own company or do you doubt your own abilities?

The more you think about overcoming the challenges in your life, of achieving goals, of looking for the good thing that might happen instead of the bad, the more likely you are to have those things happen.

You may be thinking, "Hey Russ—if thoughts matter, or if they become things, then why weren't you able to keep down your fiesta-inspired lunch that day?"

Thanks for asking!

It's true, I did throw up. Violently, and in a wide array of aesthetically displeasing shapes and colors. It was straight out of a Hollywood horror film, but with a flair only available via a Mexican fast food restaurant. I made the girl in The Exorcist look like a rookie.

But the point wasn't that I wouldn't throw up. Let's be honest—you don't pour a batch of poison directly into your body and not expect to at least have a rumbly tummy.

No, my goal was to not throw up as quickly. The fact it was Mexican food that was sure to cause me some discomfort coming back up was just raising the stakes. (Refer to previous insights about me being a teenage boy at the time.)

Which leads me to my second point: what constitutes winning? For me, in that moment, winning came in the form of waiting five minutes—300 seconds for those counting—before I stuck my head in that garbage can. It came by thinking about not throwing up when they administered the drugs. It came when I realized that thoughts become things.

If you're an athlete (or just an athletic fan) you know that a win doesn't come all at once. It comes in a series of wins. In basketball, it comes two and three points at a time. In football, it comes one touchdown or one field goal at a time. Those small wins, one right after another, leads to the big one.

When I was about four months into my chemo, my scans had come back clean. But the doctors had determined four additional months of chemo—what they called positive treatment—would be required. Although I was stronger, the treatments still took their toll on me physically. One in particular.

It was late summer in New Mexico, and I dressed for it: running shorts and a tank top—anything that would help me stay cool. I sat down to get my infusion as usual, facing the nausea and the usual after-effects. Then I got up to leave, my mother at my side to help me out to the car.

The nurse told me I needed to wait. One of the side effects of the chemo cocktail they'd just injected me with, she said, was extreme sun sensitivity. Given my choice of attire that day, they needed to cover me with blankets to protect my skin; otherwise I would feel intense burning anywhere my skin was not protected.

I was 17, I'd been told I was cancer free, and I was as invincible as I'd been in a long time. I'd kicked lung cancer's butt repeatedly, how bad would it be to get a little sun on me as I walked to the car? Filled with bravado, lacking the life experience needed to truly understand what the nurse was saying, I headed out the front door.

Then I understood it all too well.

The minute the sun hit my skin I screamed and fell to the ground. I felt as though someone had poured kerosene and lit a match to my skin. It was hard to believe that I wasn't literally on fire. I was sure if I looked at my skin I would see flames everywhere, but I didn't dare open my eyes. The nurses rushed out with blankets to shield me.

When we made it to the car I dove into the backseat. As we drove back to the house, I spent the trip on the floor, dodging sunlight, feeling as vulnerable as I could ever imagine being. I was terrified of the sun and couldn't wait to get home and hide in a dark room where its rays couldn't find me.

How was this a win? I can tell you that the next time I went in for chemo, I was ready, with sleeves and pants and a hat. I learned from that experience. I learned to ask questions about what I should expect from my treatments to prepare for them better. All of that knowledge, all of those little wins, got me to a big one.

Give yourself some credit. Realize that every experience you have is teaching you something you need to know. Give yourself a pat on the back when you achieve a goal—no matter how big it is. Think about it, and take the win.

CHAPTER ELEVEN

"We're all done here."

After 8 months, we were done with treatment. My scans remained clear. There was no need to return to the clinic.

My parents looked at me expectantly, then at the doctor. They wondered when they should schedule the follow up.

The answer was not to. Back then they didn't do three- or six- or twelve-month checkups. If I made it five years, I'd be considered cured. They wished me luck and said to call if there were any problems.

Talk about a breakup. For more than a year my life had pretty much been fighting cancer, talking to these doctors and nurses. Now they expected me to go back to high school?

It was time to resume my life.

LIFE IS WAITING.

Even though I'd decided all those months before not to die, I wasn't exactly sure how to live anymore. I went back to high school, but my experience set me apart from many of my peers.

It wasn't just the fact that I was nearly 5' 10" and a whopping 100 pounds when I went back to school. Or that I was (in whispered tones) "the kid with cancer."

No, it wasn't those things as much as I didn't want to sit still. I didn't see the point of sitting in a classroom trying to speak French when I had a bigger message to share. Not about cancer, but about life. I couldn't fly jets anymore, but I wanted to tell every person around me that life was great, that life was short, and that life mattered. I turned into an unofficial counselor, helping other students with their problems (sometimes it was more effective than others—again, I was a 17-year-old boy.)

Some teachers understood; some weren't sure what to do with me. I got to know the administration from being sent to talk with them on a fairly regular basis.

My parents tried their best to adjust to the new Russ. They were just glad to have me alive after everything I'd been through. They were one of the few who understood my "chemo brain" which made me incredibly forgetful.

Even when I left my truck in the middle of an intersection because I ran out of gas and all I could focus on was getting to school, resulting in a call from the police, my dad just made sure I was okay and then retrieved my vehicle.

Big life events—good or bad—change us. They change the way we think and feel and sometimes even the way we behave. As we learn to live again, sometimes it's hard for us to figure out what we're doing, and it's hard for those who have known us to adjust to the "new" part of us.

As a kid who'd gone from a football field to being told he was going to die to heading back to school in the space of about 16 months, I was admittedly an extreme example. Some kids who went through what I did would probably be happy to just be a high school kid again and do the things high school kids do, but I wasn't one of them. It isn't surprising people had a hard time figuring me out—heck, sometimes they still do.

If you've been through something life changing or are going through it now, know there's no road map or primer that tells you how to start living life again. I can't tell you how it should be or what you should feel. You have to figure it out for yourself.

What I can tell you is that since the day I was told my cancer treatments were over, I have embraced life. I don't take it for granted. I've had hard days, hard months and hard years since then.

I've lived through illnesses brought on by the toxicity of my treatments, and although I was clear for that five years my doctors looked for, I've had other types of cancer since then. But I wouldn't change a moment of it, because it's all been a part of becoming who I am now and helped lead me to where I am now.

Life is waiting. Don't waste even a moment not living it to its fullest.

And always, always, always remember to make room for the miracle.

About The Author

Russ Cherry has been a trainer for some of the largest companies in the world, including ExxonMobil, ConocoPhillips and Wells Fargo. He's now working to spread his message around the globe.

A two-time cancer survivor, Russ knows that every day is a good day, that without risk there are no rewards, and that people and companies can do more than merely survive—they can thrive. He knows that failure can be as much of a learning experience as success, and that asking the right question is more important than already knowing the answer. And he knows that he can help those in business—from the man on the factory floor to the CEO of a Fortune 500 Company–rediscover their own paths and unlock the doors to unqualified success.

Learn more at RussCherrySpeaks.com

From Russ Cherry's upcoming book:

THE ANGER BUCKET

Living 20 years past the date of my clean bill of health was the goal I set for myself. (Hey—when you're in your 20s, making it into your 40s seems virtually impossible whether you've had cancer or not!)

By 2008, I was still going strong, despite a few debilitating side effects due to the treatments I'd undergone in my teens. I was married to an amazing woman, had two great kids and was doing a job I loved. Everybody said I was one of the happiest guys they'd ever met.

I was speaking to a large oncology department at a regional hospital—a unit considered to the best in a four-state area. They were impressive at every level, and it was an honor when I was invited to share my story with them. My goal was to help them see how amazingly far cancer treatments had progressed since the dark ages (i.e., the 1980s).

Part of my cancer story includes a bone marrow biopsy. To this day, that biopsy was the most painful experience of my lifetime both physically and emotionally. At the same time, I treasure that experience because of what it taught me. As such, I decided to share it at the end of my presentation.

I walked them through my biopsy, moment by moment, as experienced by a skinny, scared 16-year-old boy. As I began to detail the excruciating pain I felt, you could have heard a pin drop. Until "he" spoke.

"He" was a male nurse, who decided in that moment to share his own experience.

"Come on," he said, his tone matching the roll of his eyes. "It doesn't hurt that bad. I've assisted on countless biopsies. It's a quick procedure, and not as dramatic as you're making it out to be."

The needle they used in my bone marrow biopsy is over six inches long. I know its length, because I still have that needle in my possession. Its barrel is wider than the ink barrel of a ballpoint pen, and the physician must first make an incision with a scalpel before it is used because the needle itself would cause too much damage.

I have—quite literally—seen people faint when they've seen it and heard my story. Others become sick to their stomach, and a number of them will cry. But to this man, it meant nothing.

In that moment, I lost touch with reality.

The emotions of 20 years flooded my entire system with a ferocity for which I was completely unprepared. I couldn't think. I could only feel.

I walked towards him with that needle in my hand, unable to take my eyes off of him. The rage I was feeling pounded in my ears. My arm was fully extended, and the needle was soon a few feet from his face. Only a table separated us.

"Have YOU ever had to endure this procedure?" I demanded, seething with contempt. I was shaking. "Have you?" I yelled, my voice resounding. "Have you ever had to endure it—especially from an uncaring nurse like you?"

That's when I saw the look on his face, and what I saw startled me. As I slowly became aware of my surroundings again, I realized he wasn't the only concerned person in the room. The body language of his coworkers spoke volumes.

I stepped back quickly dropped the hand holding the needle to my side. I apologized and tried to explain what came over me. I didn't want to harm him and I didn't mean to threaten him. In truth, I had no idea what had just happened.

The unit administrator, for whom I will be forever grateful, pulled me aside when my presentation was over. "Have you ever talked with anyone regarding your unresolved anger over cancer?" she asked gently.

The thought had never crossed my mind. In the 1980s nobody talked about their cancer experience and "normal" people like me had never even heard of unresolved anger.

"You need some help," she said.

For the first time in years I was speechless.

• • •

*Look for **The Anger Bucket**, coming soon.*